ChristMyths
Facts and Fictions

General Editor
Gary V Carter

Copyright © 2009 by Kainos Enterprises

All rights reserved. No part of this book may be reproduced in any form or by any electronic or mechanical means, including information storage and retrieval systems, without permission in writing from the publisher, except by a reviewer who may quote brief passages in a review.

Published By: Kainos Enterprises
                 7777 Churchville Road
                 Brampton Ontario Canada L6Y 0H3
                 905-230-8116

ISBN: 978 - 0 - 9685427 - 4 - 3

All scripture quotations, unless otherwise indicated, are taken from the HOLY BIBLE, NEW INTERNATIONAL VERSION®. NIV®. Copyright ©1973, 1978, 1984 by International Bible Society. Used by permission of Zondervan. All rights reserved.

Contributors

Christmases Past
 Fred Brown 10
Christmas In Pakistan
 Maureen Brown 14
December 25
 Heather Macdonald 16
What Christmas Means to Me
 Penelope Spears 18
The Good Old Days
 Frances Kerr 22
A Gimmer Family Tradition
 Debbie Macdonald 24
Lutefisk Plus Other Good Memories
 Wendy Carter 28
Rock & Roll Christmas
 Fred Brown 30
Christmas Is...Not Always a Happy Memory!
 Chris Burton 36
Hayley's Christmas Poem
 Hayley Macdonald 38
Shine for You
 Sara Burton 40
The Christmas Gift
 Steve Macdonald 46
The Story of the Candy Cane
 Cassidy Burton 48
A Two Way Street
 Howie Johnson 54
Jesus
 Kaiya Burton 56
God Gave
 Sara Burton and Fred Brown 62
Yeshua is Here
 Sara Burton 64

Book Introduction

Christmas has been loaded up with ChristMyths over the years. This can be very confusing without someone to help you sort it all out. Everyone needs a ChristMythBuster! That's just why we put this book together for our friends and neighbours.

The book isn't arranged like a regular book. It is a collection of personal reflections of ordinary people with some life experience to share about their thoughts and memories at Christmas time. Perhaps their stories from a wide set of perspectives and ages will bring good memories and thoughts to your mind. Every contributor participates regularly in Heartland Fellowship (The Breakfast Church).

The Breakfast Church is sort of an unchurch for many. We meet Sunday morning at 9 am for breakfast and enjoy thinking and learning, laughing and singing together. Everything is pointed to refreshing our lives as we simply focus on Jesus and the message of the Bible. No forms or rituals. No special dress – come as you are! Visitors, neighbours, friends, newcomers and observers are always welcome. We never ask anyone to speak up or do anything particularly religious. Drop by any Sunday and enjoy a coffee, muffins, fruit and some other goodies with us.

Now, back to this book. On the left hand page (even numbers) are submissions your new friends at The Breakfast Church wanted to share with you. There is no particular order. Only light editing has been done so you will know these are the real thoughts from real people you can get to know if you don't already. Every one is friendly!

On the right hand page (odd numbers) there are some items of interest in light grey boxes. Each is tagged as a fact, a fiction or perhaps an unfounded tradition. Other than those interruptions, the rest of the text flows as a unified story from beginning to end. That unified story explains where the whole Christmas thing came from and what it means in our world today. We sincerely hope this will give you some food for thought and inspiration for your life!

Hostess Introduction

Our Churchville village home was built about 1837. That's a long time ago. When neighbours or friends visit they are intrigued with the old-time construction from pioneer life. And so to highlight some of our home's unique characteristics we have been doing some renovations in one of the front rooms. A hall wall that didn't support anything was taken down to enlarge this room. After much consideration we also took down the drywall ceiling which was hiding large timbers and floorboards (some two feet wide). They have now been painted white. Our neighbours, Ross and Sarah Pengilley, had some 175 year old logs which have been cut to size and added as supporting beams. Slate ordered from China through another neighbour, Ferd Schermel, will arrive some time in December. We are excited to see the end result of our labours.

Christianity is another old time way of living that needs to be preserved and highlighted in our society particularly around the Christmas season. Not everyone holds to this belief system but we believe it is important that everyone understands what it is all about and be given the opportunity to integrate it into their lives. It must be very confusing at Christmas for newcomers to Canada – a country with a variety of religions and the freedom of each one to encourage others to join. Some come from lands where Christmas is not known and they are left on their own to figure out, for example, if Santa Claus and his reindeer, decorations on our homes, gift giving etc. are all parts of the Christian faith. Most of these fun activities are just related to the culture and tradition that have become dear to many Canadians.

We love to open our home for people to visit. We have a variety of small group events here at various times. We are always happy to meet new friends in a variety of contexts. Perhaps the easiest time for us to have a get acquainted visit is Sunday morning for breakfast at 9 am. Join us for The Breakfast Church, an informal time with lots going on! Give me or Gary a call and we will happily share a piece of our lives with you.

Wendy Carter
7777 Churchville Road
Brampton ON L6Y 0H3
905-230-8116

Christmases Past

As a child I was taught right from the beginning that there was no such person as Santa Claus. Did that ruin my excitement on Christmas morning? No, it did not. I knew that the gifts under the tree came from my parents and relatives, the people who truly love me. I remember one time near Christmas when I was around eight years old being in a friend's room playing with his toys when he asked what I wanted Santa to bring me for Christmas. I laughed at him and told him there is no such person as Santa Claus or the Easter Bunny for that matter. He got upset and ran to his dad and told him what I said. The father confirmed there was a Santa and maybe I should go home now. Gee, everyone at school believed it too. Was I the only one not converted to this secular religion?

My dad was a hard working man. His job required shift work and lots of overtime to provide for his family. He was not an emotional man and did not show his love for us in traditional ways. We still knew he did love us. He did not like the Christmas hype and was always saying "Don't get me anything for Christmas 'cause I'm not getting you anything!" I'm sure he at least gave my mom money to buy presents but for the most part I believe my mom did most of the buying. My mom worked part time as a supply teacher so she did have some money of her own. She would always save her money up so she could buy presents for us for Christmas. She enjoyed watching my brother and me tear open the nicely wrapped presents Christmas morning by the tree and shriek with glee. My mom knew it was more blessed to give than receive and it made her heart glad to see my brother and me so happy. We knew the gifts were from mom and dad – not Santa. My dad, for reasons I may never know, was not always there because sometimes he would take off up north to his parents' place in the Ottawa Valley by himself leaving us at home.

One year, as we were sitting in the living room opening our gifts on Christmas morning, our dad called us to go outside with him. He opened the garage for us to see two new bicycles for my brother and me. We screamed with delight and jumped on our new

Continued on page 10

The Real Story

You might think by the rush of activity in the month of December that Christmas is a big deal. Well, clearly it is from the perspective of north American culture and especially commercialism. As an old song of the season says, "It's the most wonderful time of the year!"

It comes as a surprise to some to find out that at its core Christianity doesn't emphasize Christmas. Christmas is a word we apply to the birth of Jesus. The "Mas" is a festival and "Christ" is the one celebrated. Actually, "Christ" isn't a name; it is a role. Think of it this way. Stephen Harper is the Prime Minister of Canada. His family name or surname is Harper and his given name or first

> ### Fact: Christmas Trees
> The practice of cutting down Christmas trees can be traced as far back as 700 A.D. A British Monk, St. Boniface, wanted to find a symbol for the Christ Child as well as move the German tribes away from the worship of the Oak Tree (a Druid practice). He introduced the fir tree in his missionary work saying, "Let this be called the tree of the Christ Child."

name is Steven. His current role is Prime Minister. Jesus was Christ's given name. He didn't have a surname. But his role is the Christ. Christ means "anointed one." Kings were anointed when their formal kingship began. Jesus is the King appointed by God. The Hebrew word meaning the same thing as the Greek word "Christ" is "Messiah" and has the concept of rescuer built in. The Hebrews, by and large, never accepted Jesus as their Messiah. Actually, there are over a hundred other names applied to Jesus in the Bible. But these are just like nicknames. Each of them gives depth of meaning to the One who is indescribable.

The only place supplying any detail whatsoever about Jesus' birth that is original and authoritative are two short documents that

Continued on page 11

Continued from page 8

bikes. We spent all day riding up and down the street. What we didn't know was that he bought these bikes as a surprise, of course, but they were also a surprise to my mom since he never told her he was getting them. My mom sat in the living-room looking at the toys she had bought for us abandoned on the floor, then looked out the window watching us ride up and down the street on our new bikes. I'm not sure what hurt more - the fact we liked the bikes more than her gifts or the fact that dad never told her he was going to buy the bikes. I know my dad never meant to hurt my mom. That was just the kind of thing he would do. He loved us.

God loves us too and wants to give us the things we pray for but He knows not all things are beneficial for us. Does God always answer our prayers? Yes, He does! But His answer is not always "yes". Sometimes He says "no" or "not right now" just like a loving parent. When we ask God for something let us always remember to say, "If it is Your will, Lord." We must not forget that God loves us and He will make His decisions wisely for us. Merry Christmas!

Fred Brown

Downtown Freddy Brown is known for his musical renditions and creativity. He performs in a variety of venues, tunes pianos and teaches music. Recently he married Maureen.

Continued from page 9

form a part of the Bible. There are 66 books bound together to make up the Bible. The Bible accepted by some portions of Christianity adds up to another 15 books, generally covering the centuries between the first part of the Bible called the Old Testament and the smaller part that follows called the New Testament. The New Testament is not a sort of revision of the Old. It is the ongoing and unfolding story of the relationship between God and man. It is new because it starts just before Jesus is born.

Only two of the New Testament books give us any detail about the birth of Jesus. There are two other books that give us great detail on Jesus' life but they do not cover the events of his birth. All told there are four books within the Bible that teach us about the life of Jesus. Two of those accounts are written by eyewitnesses of the ministry of Jesus but they weren't around when Jesus was born. The record was passed on to them – as was true with all ancient history – by word of mouth. Bear in mind that written documents didn't play the part two thousand years ago that they do today because a written document was always a handwritten document. Therefore, it took a long time to write things down and passing information by word of mouth was always accurate and convenient.

These four pieces of the New Testament are called Matthew, Mark, Luke and John. Those were the names of the authors. Matthew and John were two of the original 12 chosen by Jesus as Apostles.

John and Mark

John's accounting of the birth of Christ was very short and powerful theologically but without historical detail. His name for Jesus in chapter one is, "The Word." He firmly states, in John 1:14,

> *"The Word became flesh and made his dwelling among us. We have seen his glory, the glory of the One and Only, who came from the Father, full of grace and truth."*

Continued on page 13

Christmas In Pakistan

My youngest uncle on my mom's side would start off the Christmas season in mid-November by preparing what we called Hunter Beef. This was a very large piece of beef which was soaked in fresh lemon juice, salt and different kinds of spices. I remember that my uncle would rub it every night with fresh lemons and turn it. He did this until about the 20th of December. He would then wash off the excess salt and bake it. It was now ready to eat. You could eat it like that or lightly pan fry it. Let me tell you it was YUMMY!

It was also a tradition or custom on my mother's side of the family to bake Christmas fruit cakes. Both my oldest and youngest uncles along with my mother used to mix their own ingredients. They would make their own dough and then take it to the baker. A couple of days later my uncles would pick up at least 100 to 150 cakes from the baker.

My youngest uncle would then gather together all his nieces and nephews. We would clean out the room closest to the kitchen to make all the Christmas goodies. We really had quite an assembly line to do this! For the first batch of goodies, one person would roll out the dough, the next one would stuff it and then deliver it to the kitchen to be fried. For the next batch, one person would roll out the dough and the next person would cut it and take it to the kitchen for frying. By the time all was said and done we would have at least four to five different kinds of goodies.

The next day we all would gather again and make gift baskets with the fruit cakes, the goodies, dry fruits and oranges. These would be delivered to our Muslim neighbours and friends as Christmas gifts.

Christmas Eve was always celebrated at my youngest uncle's home. He and his wife would prepare an elaborate feast for both sides of the family and somewhere in there, Santa would arrive with gifts for everyone. The celebration would last until about midnight.

Christmas Day would begin with each family member's presence at church with all the children in new clothes – the parents' Christ-

Continued on page 14

ChristMyths – Facts and Fictions

Continued from page 11

And then he quotes, John the Baptist (a different John) who was the announcer of the start of Jesus' public ministry as an adult. John the Baptist's words recorded in John 1:17 are,

> *"This was he of whom I said, 'He who comes after me has surpassed me because he was before me."*

Then John (the writer and Apostle) says this in John 1:18-19,

> *"From the fullness of his grace we have all received one blessing after another. For the law was given through Moses; grace and truth came through Jesus Christ. No one has ever seen God, but God the One and Only, who is at the Father's side, has made him known."*

Fiction: Jesus' Birthday

Our calendar claims to measure from BC (Before Christ) to AD (Anno Domini – Latin for "In the year of Our Lord"). In actuality, somebody goofed back in 525 AD when the calculation started. Jesus was more likely born around 4 BC and most definitely it wasn't on December 25th.

That's it. Those are incredible lofty claims about Jesus but they tell us nothing about his actual birth.

Mark says even less. He starts his "Life of Jesus" with these words,

> *"The beginning of the gospel about Jesus Christ, the Son of God."*

Wow! Nothing like cutting to the chase. You know where Mark stands on who Jesus is in his first sentence.

While these two writers don't give us any insight about the birth of Jesus they certainly claim that He is unique in human history. That tells us that there is something to pay attention to and even to celebrate. Their emphasis is on actions and words of Jesus for approximately three years. The part of his life they dwell on is the last week leading up to the crucifixion, the crucifixion itself, the

Continued on page 15

Continued from page 12

mas gift to their kids. I certainly looked forward to my new Christmas dress and accessories!

After church all of us would go to the cemetery to lay flowers on the graves of our loved ones. From there it was to my oldest uncle's house for lunch.

Christmas lunch was also a big affair! My uncle used to go to a lot of trouble to prepare the meal; there would be a huge variety of different dishes to select from. The meal would last until about 6 o'clock. By this time everyone had enough to eat; then it was time to go home and relax.

This family tradition lasted until the Christmas of 1972. My mother had passed away in the summer so I went to live with my younger uncle. That was my last Christmas I celebrated with both my uncles. My older uncle migrated to the U.S. in 1973 and I moved away with my brother to another city. My brother migrated to the U.S. in 1974 and I, for the next 3 years lived with my sister-in-law and her family until I migrated to Canada in 1977.

To this day especially at Christmas time, I remember the past Christmases with my uncles and I will cherish those memories for the rest of my life.

Maureen Brown

Maureen is an accountant who lives in Brampton and works in Milton. Maureen met Fred at The Breakfast Church and in recent days married him.

Continued from page 13

resurrection and the post resurrection appearances of Jesus. Mark makes a quick reference at the end about Jesus ascending into heaven without dying again. John doesn't include that detail.

Matthew and Luke

Matthew and Luke also have the same emphases in their documents. That is, they dwell on the events of the death, burial and resurrection of Jesus after telling us some of his activities and teachings. Like John, Matthew doesn't tell us about the ascension into heaven at the end of Jesus' days on earth. However, like Mark Luke does make brief reference to that ascension.

Before we go on to the birth of Jesus and what Matthew and Luke tell us about it there is one more interesting background detail about languages. All four Gospels, as we call them, (Matthew, Mark, Luke and John) were originally written in Koine Greek or common Greek as opposed to Classical Greek. This was the most common language of the day. The actual events were conducted in Aramaic, a Hebrew dialect. But in order to spread the message far beyond the Jewish community the message was written down in Greek. We have many different English translations available today. Any one of them will suffice to get the main message across. Translators are concerned with meaning exchange from the original language to the new language. And they all do a pretty good job of keeping their biases and interpretations out of their work. So you can pick up any Bible you want and get the same thrust.

Matthew's Christmas

Now let's get to the main events. This is how we are going to handle it. We will go through the message of Matthew and Luke and quote what they say about the birth of Jesus interspersed with some explanatory material. The only time italics is used here is

Continued on page 17

December 25

Every year on December twenty-five
We celebrate; our homes come alive
With lights and trees and gifts to give.
This says Christ is born, so that we may live.

Jesus and Santa, do we compare
Suit of red, or a Saviour so fair?
Pretty gifts, sitting under the tree
Or a life in Heaven for eternity?

Away in the manger, a new babe is born
King of Kings, Lord of Lords.
His gift is His life, to save you and me.
He gave it to us at Calvary.

Son, on Christmas day as you open your gifts
Remember the manger; it's not about lists.
He hung on a tree with a crown of thorns.
Is it all about this day he was born?

Or something beyond the gifts and the fun?
It is about the gift from God's only Son.
HE came to earth on that day long ago.
He gave life eternal to those that know.

Heather Macdonald

Heather is a high school student. She gets great marks, plays the flute and is on the school lacrosse team.

Continued from page 15

where the Bible is being quoted directly. The rest of the material is uninspired but I hope inspiring!

Matthew starts the history lesson this way in Matthew 1:18.

"This is how the birth of Jesus Christ came about: His mother Mary was pledged to be married to Joseph, but before they came together, she was found to be with child through the Holy Spirit. Because Joseph her husband was a righteous man and did not want to expose her to public disgrace, he had in mind to divorce her quietly."

Fiction: Santa Claus

Santa Claus, also known as Saint Nicholas, Father Christmas, Kris Kringle or simply "Santa", is an imaginary figure who, in many Western cultures, brings gifts to the homes of the good children during the late evening and overnight hours of Christmas Eve, December 24 or in some places December 6.

Some Christians resist teaching the fantasy of Santa lest it be confused with the historical reality of Jesus. They also want to avoid the child's disappointment when they find out the truth. Others think this robs the child of a fun part of the Christmas celebrations.

Joseph and Mary had never had sex. They knew it if nobody else did. But Joseph assumed that Mary was telling a lie and had become pregnant by another man. He wanted to make the best of the situation and break the pledge of marriage by divorcing her. The marriage pledge was much more binding than engagements are today. Joseph wanted to let Mary move on and perhaps become a single mom or marry the other man and tell whatever story she liked. That would be much easier in the day than dealing with the idea of a pregnancy before marriage.

But after he had considered this, an angel of the Lord appeared to him in a dream and said,

Continued on page 19

What Christmas Means to Me

When I was a child, what Christmas meant to me was getting excited about the Santa Claus Parade every year. I would then know that Christmas was almost here. The Santa Clause parade would march right past my house on Dupont Street in Toronto. We had a closed-in veranda so we didn't have to bundle up to keep warm; however my grandma still always gave us all hot chocolate.

After the parade a bunch of us would go down to Honest Ed's Department Store as Santa would be there. We could sit on his knee and whisper in his ear what it was that we wanted for Christmas. As I got a little older I really enjoyed being in the choir at church. Several of us who were in the choir always had a role to play or we would sing together as a whole. What I really liked, though, was getting to sing solo. One of my favourite Christmas carols was "Away in a Manger."

Although my Grandma bought us presents, she made sure that we knew what Christmas was really about which was the celebration of our Lord Jesus Christ, our Saviour.

Since I have become a mother, I have always tried to make sure my son understood this meaning of Christmas and the difference between Santa Claus and Jesus Christ.

Penelope Spears

Penny is a mother to Brandon and works in an accounting department in a local Mississauga business.

ChristMyths – Facts and Fictions

Continued from page 17

> *"Joseph son of David, do not be afraid to take Mary home as your wife, because what is conceived in her is from the Holy Spirit. She will give birth to a son, and you are to give him the name Jesus, because he will save his people from their sins."*

In a Dream

Joseph has a dream. It was a dream including an angel with a message. The angel declares the totally improbable. There is no human father. This is a miracle of the Holy Spirit. Now, we can't take the time here to go into all the detail but this brings into play the unfolding of what subsequently has become known as the teaching of the Trinity. The Trinity in Christian revelation is God the Father, God the Son (Jesus) and God the Holy Spirit. But right here it doesn't say anything about this. The passage does introduce the word, *"Lord."* This is the name for God which in Hebrew had four letters YHWH but was never pronounced. We have seen it transliterated by adding some vowels as Yahweh or Jehovah. Think if it as the name of God that reveals to us not only his greatness as the Creator and Ultimate Authority in the universe. The name declares that this Ultimate One is intimately concerned about the affairs of people and takes great pains to set up lines of communication and help for all people on earth. His chosen vehicle for blessing the whole world is the Hebrew nation or ethnic group.

Thus, the message portrayed here is that there is One God who sends a messenger to tell Joseph that something world shaping is about to occur. The angel tells Joseph that the baby has been pre-named. The name of the baby is Jesus. That name means *"Saviour."* Thus the following explanation, *"because he will save his people from their sins."* The message is quite clear but absolutely incredible. Mary, without Joseph having any advance warning, is pregnant without a human father. Apparently Joseph had no hunch that there was anything special about Mary. He concluded that divorce was the only option until he got his jolt from the angel in his dream.

Continued on page 21

The Good Old Days

In the 1930s (the depression years) Christmas was very different.

There was very little money to buy gifts; we made quite a few items as presents. Little children knew that hanging a stocking would give them some candy and perhaps an orange. Fruit was hard to get, especially oranges. We did enjoy getting our stockings on Christmas morning. If we were lucky there might be a book or small puzzle included.

I remember one Christmas when my sister was about four years old. She was hoping she might get a doll from Santa. Santa was still believed in as bringing presents. That was the year that made me realize that Christmas was Christ's birthday.

It happened this way. My sister had a girlfriend who lived next door. On Christmas morning my sister went to visit her to take her some of her Christmas candy. What my sister saw at that house was truly amazing. There was a doll in a little baby buggy as well as a large doll sitting beside a great pile of presents. When my sister came home, she was crying.

When we got her tears wiped away and she was able to tell us what was wrong, this is what she said. "I have been a good girl all year (and this was true) and yet Santa brought me only one little doll and some candy. He brought all those things to Ruth and she was a very naughty girl that did not even go to Sunday School." We had a little talk with her right then to let her know that there really wasn't a Santa.

It was really mothers and dads who bought stuff for their kids. Santa was just a story told at Christmas time. The thing that made a big difference in my life was when my little sister looked up at us and asked, "Is Jesus real?" I made up my mind that I would not teach my children to believe in Santa.

Sure, we went to visit the stores and looked at the many items for sale but both my boys knew that mothers and fathers bought the stuff that they got at Christmas. We spent more time on the real

Continued on page 22

Continued from page 19

Then Matthew adds something for his primarily Hebrew audience as he writes,

> *"All this took place to fulfill what the Lord had said through the prophet: 'The virgin will be with child and will give birth to a son, and they will call him Immanuel' – which means, 'God with us.'"*

Matthew is quoting from a respected prophet Isaiah. Isaiah 7:14 is where he gets his quote about the coming virgin birth. But Isaiah had written this over 700 years previously. They had to wait all this time for the fulfillment. And make no mistake this Son is declared to be God. God with us. That is God in a human body. This is the promise of the God-Man. The One and Only that John mentioned.

Fact: Christmas Carols Banned

Oliver Cromwell banned the singing of Christmas Carols from 1640 to 1660 because he believed that Christmas should be a very solemn event. There would be no parties because the day should only be observed by a sermon and a prayer service.

Getting Married

The story goes on.

> *"When Joseph woke up, he did what the angel of the Lord had commanded him and took Mary home as his wife. But he had no union with her until she gave birth to a son. And he gave him the name Jesus."*

Joseph believed the angelic message. He immediately married Mary. But at the same time they never had sex until after the birth of Jesus. The statement clearly implies that life as a married couple was normalized after the birth of Jesus. In fact, later in his document Matthew names four brothers of Jesus that followed him into the family, James, Joseph, Simon and Judas. (Matthew

Continued on page 23

Continued from page 20

Christmas stories, the birth of the baby in Bethlehem and the gifts that the wise men brought. Our Christmases were every bit as happy as if there were piles of presents and we rejoiced in knowing a loving Saviour.

Frances Kerr

An octogenarian who loves to teach children about the Bible. She is also an accomplished magician.

Continued from page 21

13:55). This naming thing gets complicated in the Bible because, much as today, many people were given the same name. But just to be clear this James does show up later in the Bible; Joseph was apparently named after his father; Simon was also the original name of Peter, the apostolic leader, but that is not this Simon and of course, Judas is not the one of the 12 who betrayed Jesus in the end.

The Name

The main point so far is that they did as they were instructed and gave the baby the name "Jesus."

> ### Fiction: Taking Christ Out of Christmas
>
> The idea that "X" replaced "Christ" in Christmas as a way to secularize the holiday isn't true at all. The "X" is an early church substitute for the Greek "Chi" which represents the first letters for the spelling of Christ.

Incidentally the verse and chapter divisions in the Bible were added in the middle ages and continue to be used by convention but they were never part of the original documents. So the document just keeps moving without chapter or even sentence or paragraph divisions. They didn't use punctuation. We need it so it can make sense to us.

The next words introduce a new part of the story.

> *"After Jesus was born in Bethlehem in Judea, during the time of King Herod, Magi from the east came to Jerusalem and asked, 'Where is the one who has been born king of the Jews? We saw his star in the east and have come to worship him.'"*

Continued on page 25

A Gimmer Family Tradition

For as long as I can remember my family has celebrated the holidays in the same way.

The kids would wake up and ask, "Can we open our stockings now?"

The answer has always been the same, "Not yet – we need to thank Someone first."

So the tradition starts and we voice a prayer to God to say thank you for the greatest gift anyone could ever have received – the giving of His Son just for us and for helping us get through another year.

The second part to our tradition is to have a bacon and egg breakfast before gift time. My family has tried to carry both parts of this tradition over into the next generation with minor alterations.

We might not eat the breakfast every year as we all travel from our own homes.

My biggest hope is that as our children grow and have families of their own it is just as important for them to remember that gift giving is not the most important part of the holidays.

Debbie Macdonald

Debbie works from home on many fronts. She volunteers with the Girl Guides. Debbie is Steve's wife and mother of Heather and Hayley.

Continued from page 23

Bethlehem

We start off by learning the town in which Jesus was born. Bethlehem is of course famous today. But its main claim to fame in that day rested on the fact that the esteemed King David had also been born there about a thousand years earlier. And in fact, one passage from the prophet Micah written 700 years earlier had predicted this in Micah 5:2,

> *"But you, Bethlehem Ephrathah, though you are small among the clans of Judah, out of you will come for me one who will be ruler over Israel, whose origins are from of old, from ancient times."*

Micah foresaw a coming ruler over all Israel that was to come from the tribe of Judah. Amazingly, he pinpointed the village of his birth. Even more amazingly, he suggests that the origins of this ruler were from ancient times. That is he gives indication that this ruler existed before coming to Bethlehem.

Herod

Let's talk about Herod. He was a domineering king over the area. In fact, from Bethlehem you could see his magnificent mountain top retreat. The ruins are still there today. Herod did some good things in terms of public works in the area but he wasn't about to share his throne. He got the message of a rising rivalry from that Micah prophecy and he was going to have none of it. To what extent would he go? Just wait for it.

The Magi

Somehow the Magi figured it out. These astrologers from the east had travelled to follow what they believed to be some kind of omen or announcement in this unusual star. We don't know how far east they came from but perhaps it was near Babylon in current day Iraq. The nature of this star is a mystery to us but it wasn't to them. They were compelled to go after this moving object until it came to the area near Jerusalem. They obviously had possession of

Continued on page 27

Lutefisk Plus Other Good Memories

So what is Lutefisk you ask? My Swedish parents enjoyed white fish that had been pickled in lye for a couple of months before Christmas and then cooked to accompany boiled potatoes and a white sauce spiced with nutmeg. I loved the smell in our house from this Christmas Eve tradition but I didn't like the actual taste of the fish.

My immediate family opened presents Christmas Eve under a beautifully lit Christmas tree. We enjoyed Christmas breakfast with my mom's cheese dreams (cheese and bacon on bread grilled in the oven) and coffee bread.

Are you old enough to remember seeing a pen wiper around your house? When my sister was young she made one of these at school. It was a round, yellow double-layered circle made of felt with a button in the middle. In those days the common writing tool was a pen with a nib that was dipped in a bottle of ink. She gifted this one to our ever fun-loving Uncle Bob at our extended family's Christmas dinner. The next year she received it back as a gift. It became the question of the day for several years – whose turn was to receive the infamous pen wiper specially wrapped up or some how disguised for the occasion? These are all part of the list of good memories from my childhood days and beyond.

Around the age of twenty, my father had become a soldier in his homeland of Finland. One night he found himself drunk in a ditch and decided that was not the life for him. A few years later my parents met each other as immigrants in Canada, married and set up a Christian home in Toronto.

My dad died at the age of 99 in December of 2007; my mom followed a few months later at the age of 95. I am so grateful for their long-lasting, purposeful marriage. I never had to live in fear in a home where there was alcohol abuse or divisive relationships. Their love and peace based on their genuine Christian faith was passed along to me to consider for my own life.

Continued on page 28

Continued from page 25

a copy of Micah's document. And they got the message. They came to Jerusalem and asked about this new King of the Jews.

However, nobody in town had a clue that this king was on the scene. You would have to presume that they thought they were the last to know and that everyone in Jerusalem was talking about this

Fact: The Ancient Record

The John Ryland's fragment is a fragment from a papyrus document measuring only 8.9 by 6 cm. The front contains lines from the Gospel of John 18:31–33 in Greek and the back contains lines from verses 37–38.

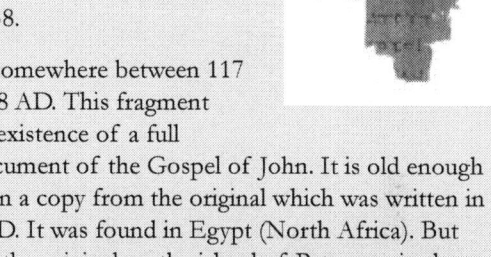

It is dated somewhere between 117 AD and 138 AD. This fragment proves the existence of a full original document of the Gospel of John. It is old enough to have been a copy from the original which was written in about 90 AD. It was found in Egypt (North Africa). But John wrote the original on the island of Patmos – in the Aegean Sea. We don't know how or when it got to Egypt.

This points to the dissemination and accuracy of Bible manuscript transmission unparalleled in human history.

great event and special King. These men from the east weren't kings as expressed in the old Christmas carol and we don't know that there were three of them from the Bible. They were men of significance who sought to guide the society by reading messages in the skies and apparently cross referencing with sacred docu-

Continued on page 29

Continued from page 26

In 1968 Gary and I were married establishing our own Christian home. We raised four children who are now all married and living in various parts of Canada. And no, the lutefisk tradition did not get passed along. However, a few years ago we started a new tradition. We decided as a family not to exchange gifts as adults any more but to take the money we would have spent and donate it to a charity of our choice.

Traditions have come and gone but our foundational belief in Jesus Christ, God's Son remains the same day after day and will remain until those who place their trust in Jesus take our last breath and go to meet him in heaven.

Wendy Carter

Wendy is an accomplished writer. She shares four children and eight grandchildren with Gary. In her spare time she gardens and reads.

ments. Their presence in town was notable and the news got to King Herod.

When King Herod heard this he was disturbed, and all Jerusalem with him. When he had called together all the people's chief priests and teachers of the law, he asked them where the Christ was to be born.

Fact and Fiction: Holly

In northern Europe, since this plant remained green throughout the harsh winters, boughs were placed over the doors of homes to drive away evil. It was also brought indoors to freshen the air and brighten the mood during the long winter. Legend has said that the holly sprang from the footsteps of Christ as he walked the earth. The pointed leaves represented the crown of thorns He wore on the cross and the red berries symbolized the blood He shed.

"In Bethlehem in Judea," they replied, "for this is what the prophet has written:" 'But you, Bethlehem, in the land of Judah, are by no means least among the rulers of Judah; for out of you will come a ruler who will be the shepherd of my people Israel.'"

Rivals

Herod saw a rival and he was upset about it. The rest of the city got upset as well because they didn't need to see Herod go haywire again. There was no telling what he would do once he smelled a threat. Herod gathered his religious advisers together to research this thing about a new King in waiting. They nailed it. As good advisers would do, they told Herod about the Micah prophecy.

Then Herod called the Magi secretly and found out from them the exact time the star had appeared. He sent them to Bethlehem and said,

Rock & Roll Christmas

I don't remember Santa Claus dying in my place
Just sliding down a chimney into a fireplace.
He may have brought me presents but never saved my soul
So I'll believe in Jesus, He's the Rock that doesn't roll.

> So, if you want a reason to celebrate this season
> Believe, (believe), Believe, (believe)
> Believe on the name of the Lord!

He's s'posed to be all knowing as in "if you're good or bad".
If you disobey your parents, it really makes him sad.
He loves the little children and sits them on his knee
Sounds a little like a fisherman from Galilee.

The red suit makes me think of the blood Christ shed for me,
The white beard and the trimmings, of Jesus' purity.
I think I understand now how Santa came to be
You can think of Santa or reality.

Fred Brown

ChristMyths – Facts and Fictions

Continued from page 29

> *"Go and make a careful search for the child. As soon as you find him, report to me, so that I too may go and worship him."*

By now if you didn't already know the story you have figured out that Herod is as sly as a fox. He has no intention of worshipping the new King. That should be obvious. But at first it appears these

> ### Tradition: The Twelve Days
>
> The Twelve Days of Christmas are the festive days beginning on Christmas Day and ending on the evening of the Twelfth Day of Christmas. The tradition appears to have started in the Middle Ages. This period was one of continuous feasting and merrymaking.
>
> The common festive song was first published in 1780. But before then Shakespeare popularized the 12 days with his play Twelfth Night which was written about 1600.

Magi cooperate with his agenda. There is an interesting note here about when the star appears. Herod needed to know that fact for his future planning. As we will see in a moment, some months have transpired from the actual birth of Jesus until these unfolding events.

The Star

> *"After they had heard the king, they went on their way, and the star they had seen in the east went ahead of them until it stopped over the place where the child was. When they saw the star, they were overjoyed. On coming to the house, they saw the child with his mother Mary, and they bowed down and worshiped him. Then they opened their treasures and presented him with gifts of gold and of incense and of myrrh. And having been warned in a dream not to go back to Herod, they returned to their country by another route."*

Continued on page 33

Christmas Is…Not Always a Happy Memory!

December 25th, 1998 was a day that I had been looking forward to for many years. My wife, Sara, myself, and our soon to be born child would be celebrating our first Christmas. I was looking forward to a joyous time as we toured from family to family sharing this great event.

Christmas had always been a fun, if not exciting time in my life. My parents had divorced and both had remarried so that meant there were a lot of people and places to visit during the holiday season. It was busy, yet enjoyable. Each year we would hang our stockings by the fireplace. Yes, we really did have a fireplace. We would often have a fire on Christmas Eve but we always had to make sure the fire was out before bedtime because we didn't want to set Santa on fire. We'd place cookies and some carrots on a plate and leave some milk for Santa, then head to bed with great expectations for the following morning. The next morning we'd spend the day in our PJ's playing with our new toys and having a great time.

Boxing day was often spent travelling to our Omi's (Grandma's) home in Waterloo for a Christmas gathering with cousins. There was always too much to eat; however we some how managed to stuff ourselves and still find room for more. There would be more games and gifts and lots of laughter. The one thing that stands out the most, though, was the time we'd spend together singing Christmas carols. Those were some great memories.

As I grew up the gatherings continued but Christmas became less about the toys and more about the celebration of the birth of our Saviour, Jesus. We'd go to a Christmas Eve service to see the plays and sing some carols. It wasn't so much about Santa any more and all the gifts, but the gift of the Son of God.

Years passed and I was married, living in Japan with Sara. After three wonderful years of experiences we decided it was time to return home; we wanted to start a family. We returned home, baby

Continued on page 34

ChristMyths – Facts and Fictions

Continued from page 31

This part of the story contains some great imagery. You will see this played out in scenes on lawns and even in public parks. But they don't have it exactly right. When we get to Luke's separate account you will clearly understand this. The Magi find the location of this ruler by following the star the short distance from Jerusalem to Bethlehem. And the star stops moving over the exact location of Jesus. They find him with Mary in a house. Not a barn. Not a cave. But a house. The other part of the story from Luke has been blended in with the current expression of things but not the clear declarations of the history. The Magi or Wise Men never saw Jesus in a manger. They brought their gifts to Jesus in the house. Three gifts are mentioned – all of the gifts were precious

> ### Fact: The First North American Carol
>
> Jesus Ahatonhia was a Huron carol written by St. John de Brébeuf, a Jesuit missionary linguist who had worked among the Huronian Indians from 1626. He was tortured and burned at the stake by Iroquois Indians in 1649. This carol written in the Huron language and put to a 16th century folk song was preserved by those Huronians who were able to escape and settle in Loretto, Quebec. In 1749 the song was rediscovered, translated into English and in 1926 reworded by Edgar Middleton. Google Jesus Ahatonhia to read the words.

and costly. They worshipped Jesus while Mary apparently looked on. That is about it. We don't know what they said or what they asked. We don't even know if Joseph was in on the discussion if there even was a discussion.

We don't know how long they stayed. But we do have a clue. One or more of these men were warned in a dream that they should not complete their contract with Herod. They should just get back on the road and go home without talking to Herod. So we can

Continued on page 35

Continued from page 32

on board, so to speak, and looked forward to the next stage in our lives. It should have been a joyous event. It should have been the best days of our lives. It was neither; however it certainly was and is a time that neither of us will ever forget.

March 27th, 1998 was going to be a day to remember. We had called the family to let them know we were on the way to the hospital because Sara was ready to give birth. What we thought was going to happen was far from what really happened. The doctors couldn't find a heart beat – our baby was dead. We'd discover later that sometime during the night the cord had become wrapped around the baby's neck and she had died. My wife was going to delivery our first child – a stillborn.

Kacie was her name, and despite her passing she was still a beautiful baby. I would never see her look me in the eyes wondering who I was. I would never hear her laugh or cry and I would never see her smile. She was Daddy's girl.

As you can imagine it was not an easy time for Sara and me. The following days, weeks and months were a blur of emotions. Through it all, though, we trusted in God. We knew that He had not abandoned us. We weren't being punished for anything, but just because we called Christ, our Saviour, didn't mean we got a free pass from life's tragedies. It's just part of life and it happens to all of us sooner or later.

December 25th, 1998 should have been the best Christmas ever; it was the worst. As the weeks leading up to Christmas came and went each Sunday I would see all the other dads with their kids. I would be reminded that this Christmas I would only be left with an empty feeling, a void where my Kacie should be.

Since that time I have been blessed with three more wonderful girls and Christmas for them holds many of the same wonders and expectations that I had as a child. It's even more joyous knowing that my girls understand that Jesus is the real reason for the season. As for me, I can't experience Christmas or its carols without feeling the void in my life where my Kacie should be. Yes,

Continued on page 36

Continued from page 33

guess that they spent at least one night in Bethlehem before packing up and hitting the road.

Fact: Swaddling Clothes

From the Gospel of Luke (2:6, 12) in the New Testament we learn that when Jesus was born, Mary, His mother wrapped Him in cloths before placing Him in a manger. An older version of the Bible describes these cloths as "swaddling." So do you know what "swaddling" means? According to Wikipedia, this was an "age-old practice of wrapping infants snugly in swaddling cloths, blankets or similar cloth so that movement of the limbs is tightly restricted" which resulted in proper posture. This practice was looked upon favourably throughout the ensuing centuries (except during the 17th century due to the neglect of proper baby care), even up until the day we now live in where it has become standard in many hospitals along with putting the baby to sleep on its back. Studies have proven that babies sleep better and longer with modern swaddling. The risk of sudden infant death syndrome may also be lowered. This practice provides a great transition from the womb to the outside world. There are so many good things we can learn from history, particularly from the Bible.

We're Outta Here

Now the story gets tense.

> *"When they had gone, an angel of the Lord appeared to Joseph in a dream. 'Get up,' he said, 'Take the child and his mother and escape to Egypt. Stay there until I tell you, for Herod is going to search for the child to kill him.' So he got up, took the child and his mother during the night and left for Egypt, where he stayed until the death of Herod. And so was fulfilled what the Lord had said through the prophet: 'Out of Egypt I called my son.'"*

Continued on page 37

ChristMyths – Facts and Fictions

Continued from page 34

Christmas is a reminder of the day that God decided to put in motion the greatest of all plans for our salvation by giving us His Son, Jesus. But for me it is also a reminder of the loss of my first child.

My faith, my church, my wife and my kids keep me going, but mostly I look forward to the day that I will be able to see my Kacie again – to hold her and look her in the eyes and maybe even get a little smile.

Chris Burton

Chris (shown here with his brother Ron) is a school teacher and loves sports. He and Sara have three children, Cassidy, Kaiya and Carleigh.

ChristMyths – Facts and Fictions

Continued from page 35

Joseph has another dream. This time the angel tells him that Herod wants to kill the child. Joseph is to move his family of three a long way out of Herod's line of sight. They are to move to Egypt. This is what they did. As refugees they left in the middle of the night and went south to Egypt. Some time later they came back and set up normal family life in Nazareth – a town a fair distance north of Bethlehem and Jerusalem.

> ### Fact: Jesus' Mission
>
> According to Luke 19:10, Jesus described the reason he came this way, *"For the Son of Man came to seek and to save what was lost."* He believed that people are lost and his role was to seek such people out and save them. Thus, there are two kinds of people according to Jesus – saved and lost. What category do you belong in?

How Could He?

And the story gets gruesome.

> *"When Herod realized that he had been outwitted by the Magi, he was furious, and he gave orders to kill all the boys in Bethlehem and its vicinity who were two years old and under, in accordance with the time he had learned from the Magi."*

This unconscionable act of murder with all the boys in the area shows us something of Herod's true character. But of course, he failed to kill the correct child. The clue here is that he killed all the boys under two years. That would give us clear evidence that this whole event happened when Jesus was somewhere between the age of one and two. Jesus was definitely not a young baby by the time the Magi arrived. He was probably walking around and playing in the house as toddlers normally do.

That is all Matthew tells us about the early life of Jesus. Out of those facts all manner of fictitious embellishments have been added over the years. It is not so unusual for people to want to fill

Continued on page 39

Hayley's Christmas Poem

When He was born, He was called Jesus.
When I was born, I was called Hayley.
He was the King of kings;
I am one of His followers.

He was baptized by John.
I was baptized by Gary.
We both have and have had friends.
Some betrayed us, others stuck by us.
He has gone through ups and downs,
And I still am going through them.

Jesus is my Saviour;
He is our Saviour!
Jesus has given and gotten.
Just like us, He gave His life for us
And He had it given back.

When we give something for Christmas,
We don't always remember that.
All we think is that was expensive,
And I hope they like it.

So let's all stop during this season
And remember what He has given us.

Hayley Macdonald

Hayley is a daughter to Steve and Debbie and sister to Heather. She is a fun-loving teenager.

Continued from page 37

in the details of the story. But it is important for us to know the history so that when we see some story book or movie that we know the raw story has been enhanced. Those enhancements are usually added one at a time to make the story speak strongly. Unfortunately, for some who aren't students of the Bible or history things have become garbled. But now you know!

> ### Tradition: Wreaths
>
> Wreaths have been used for various purposes dating back to about 800 BC. While there were forerunners in Europe, it is believed by many that the modern day Christmas wreath originated in the American colonies. A homemade wreath would be fashioned from local greenery. Making the wreaths was one of the traditions of Christmas Eve to be hung on the door for the next 12 days. Many different symbols have been seen in the wreath supplying some spiritual significance. These are understood differently in many Christian traditions.
>
> While there is no certain meaning or origin to the wreath, they do look nice on a door during the Christmas season.

The second incident from the early life of Jesus is entirely separate and is recorded for us by Luke. There is complete harmony between the two records. Luke has a different purpose in writing his story. Even though it comes in the third book of the New Testament the events we are about to cover are sort of like a prequil to the facts declared by Matthew.

Luke's Christmas

Luke begins his Gospel with this interesting statement of purpose and method.

> *"Many have undertaken to draw up an account of the things that have been fulfilled among us, just as they were handed down to us*

Continued on page 41

Shine for You

You are the light (echo) Light of the world (echo)
A city of light (echo) The Spirit of Truth (echo)
Shine, Shine, Shine, Shine.

You saved us from the night.
You filled us with Your light.
Use us to light the way to You.

We are the light (echo) Light of the world (echo)
A city of Light (echo) With Your Spirit of truth (echo)
Shine, shine, shine, shine.

You placed us high on a hill.
Like a City in the night
We open our eyes and we shine for You.

At Christmas time (echo) When we turn on the lights (echo)
We remember the light (echo) That You sent down to earth (echo)
Shine, shine, shine, shine.

You came to earth as a man —
A baby born in a barn.
You came to light the way to You.

Sara Burton

Sara is a Regional Manager of Group Exercise for GoodLife Fitness. She is married to Chris and they run a busy household with three daughters and Chris's brother Ron. Sara has composed much of the music sung at The Breakfast Church.

by those who from the first were eyewitnesses and servants of the word. Therefore, since I myself have carefully investigated everything from the beginning, it seemed good also to me to write an orderly account for you, most excellent Theophilus, so that you may know the certainty of the things you have been taught."

Fact: The First Christmas Card

In the year 1843, Sir Henry Cole wanted to send more Christmas greetings than he had time to write, so he commissioned John Calcott Horsley to paint a card for him. Notice that he wanted to show the plight of the needy beside a picture of merriment. Legend says Sir Henry didn't send any cards the following year, but the custom became popular anyway.

We do not know who this target recipient Theophilus is. But it is not uncommon in any age for one to write a book with a particular person in mind even though wider circulation is also intended. We don't know who the "many" are that Luke refers to. We don't have those documents or accounts available to us other than those written by Matthew, Mark and John. John's record did not exist at the time Luke was writing so we are down to two of the many that he is referring to. You may recall that Matthew and John were two of the eyewitness written accounts. Therefore, the only remaining written eyewitness account that Luke had at his disposal could have been Matthew. And we don't know that for sure. However, he did have the tools of investigative journalism and historical research. He states unequivocally that he carefully investigated the facts. This implies that of these other attempts to write things down, the authors had messed things up. Thankfully we don't have

The Christmas Gift

At this time of year, everything seems to take on a special meaning. There seems to be more reasons to get together with friends and family, special meals, parties with coworkers and all of these gatherings tend to create memories which stay with us for our lifetime.

Sadly I do not remember a single birthday present but I can remember the Big Bruiser tow truck I got one year for Christmas. It was massive, it was fun, and I was the envy of my friends. The Stuka gas powered airplane which I pined for endlessly and promptly crashed into the ground mere hours after I opened it – never to fly again. Ask my wife and children if I still ask for the Electronic Battleship game which was not under the tree one year. They will no doubt answer, "Constantly!"

These toys and many more hold a special place within me as do other things associated with Christmas – my mother's Christmas cookies; that terrible silver aluminum tree we had to have for a few years in the 60s; opening the stockings in my sister's bedroom to allow mom and dad a few extra minutes of sleep; the agonizing wait until dad got up and went to the living-room before we could go and check out the presents under the tree; the equally agonizing spotlights dad used with his Super 8 camera to illuminate the room and blind his children.

I remember being distraught when Bing Crosby died. "No Bing" meant no television specials which I associated with no more Christmases. Fortunately, we still had Andy Williams and his Christmas albums – one red and one green cover. I now own the CD for one of them and every year I scan all the bargain bins in the hope of finding the other one.

Does everyone have the Rankin's claymation Christmas videos? We do and watch them repeatedly each year. Tim Allen and the Santa Claus movies will surely be a staple in my daughters' future. Their children will no doubt sit with their parents and watch with mild amusement as they relive Christmases past.

Continued on page 44

Continued from page 41

those documents because they didn't stand the test of contemporary scrutiny. Nobody bothered to copy their poorly constructed documents.

But Luke is different. The detail in Luke's writing in both the Gospel of Luke and subsequently the record of the early church in the Book of Acts had been proven over time to be impeccably accurate. Luke is very precise with his history. He was willing to put his work out there under peer scrutiny among the eyewitnesses and it passed the test with flying colours. His work was widely circulated as part of the accurate standard of the events the writings cover.

> ### Fiction: Rudolph the Red Nosed Reindeer
>
> Rudolph the Red-Nosed Reindeer is a relative newcomer to Christmas tradition. The character was created in a story and song by the same name. The story was created by Robert L. May in 1939 as part of his employment with Montgomery Ward. Gene Autry recorded it formally in 1949, and it has since filtered into the popular consciousness. It made it to #1 on the charts for one week only at Christmas that same year.

Now we will jump over some of the important early stories in his book in order to get to the birth of Jesus starting at Luke 1:26,

> "...God sent the angel Gabriel to Nazareth, a town in Galilee, to a virgin pledged to be married to a man named Joseph, a descendant of David. The virgin's name was Mary. The angel went to her and said, 'Greetings, you who are highly favored! The Lord is with you.'"

In Matthew the story is accurately told of another angel visitation in a dream to Joseph. Here the angel has a name, Gabriel. We don't know if this is the same angel sent to Joseph. There is no mention here of the angel visiting Mary in a dream. Mary was highly

Continued on page 45

ChristMyths – Facts and Fictions

Continued from page 42

So many things which bring a special feeling of warmth, love, and peace remind us of good things. When our families were together we shared gifts and food and we shared love.

With all the things I can remember and still hold dear in my heart about Christmas, with all the things I still do year after year to try and maintain the mystery and magic of this time of year, I must admit that a few years ago, the gifts, the trees, the music, the gatherings began to wane in importance. What was once the focus, the apex of the year changed and began to shift. No longer is Christmas the ultimate holiday for me. Yes, I do enjoy all the festivities that are associated with this time of year, but my attention has shifted to the one gift that I unknowingly have wished for since I first became aware of the manger. It was a gift that was not wrapped up in colourful paper; it was a gift that was not in a letter or a magazine. This gift was not found after countless hours in a crowded mall or at the expense of going into debt because it was too expensive. This gift came with music more beautiful than either Bing or Andy could ever hope to produce. This gift came with a price tag I could never hope to pay.

This gift was the Living Son of God, born to die for me. He did not have to check any list to know if I was "naughty or nice." He knew the answer already; yet He gave me a gift that I cannot break or discard if it is too small. There is nothing I can do but accept His gift and if possible re-gift it to others. Not just at Christmas time, but every day.

This gift changed my focus from celebrating Christmas to celebrating another holiday – a holiday which meant absolutely nothing to me until I received His gift. Easter is my Christmas! Yes, the birth of Jesus is now significant to me; however that is like a gift within a bigger gift to me. What happened at Calvary, what happened three days later, that is the true gift that was given to me and that I celebrate not once a year, but every day.

Will my children remember Christmas videos and special songs which come out for one month each year? I hope so because they

Continued on page 46

Continued from page 43

favoured. That is, she was chosen to be the one to bear the Messiah as the angel is about to declare.

Mary doesn't play a big role in the New Testament story. She is only mentioned a few times throughout. Joseph falls out of the story almost completely. We don't know if he died at a young age. We do know that Mary was at the foot of the cross and probably lived on for some years after Jesus went back to heaven. Mary was a common name in the Gospels. However, outside the stories in Matthew and Luke the name Mary usually refers to a different person than the mother of Jesus. The only other place Mary the mother of Jesus is mentioned occurs when Luke explains in Acts

> ### Tradition: Jingle Bells
> While Jingle Bells is not technically tied to Christmas it certainly is in the minds of many. It was originally written by a minister for use in a Thanksgiving program at his church in 1857. It was so much fun and so well accepted that it lives on today in those who have never even seen a one horse open sleigh!

chapter one that she was with the disciples at the beginning of the evolution of the church. The Apostle Paul, the prolific writer of the New Testament never mentions her name. Just as an aside, if you want to check facts like these please do! One easy way to do that is by going to www.BibleGateway.com and using their extensive search functions to look up words such as "Mary" to confirm that what is written here is the truth.

Now back to Luke's unfolding story. Mary's reaction to this greeting was predictable. She knew that she wasn't so special – at least up until now – and that the angel was up to something more.

Mary was greatly troubled at his words and wondered what kind of greeting this might be. But the angel said to her,

Continued on page 47

Continued from page 44

are good memories. What will they remember? Special cookies, family gatherings and parties – all are nice memories and some stories to tell their children. Will they understand about the gift their mom and I spent hours trying to find and the relief we felt when it was wrapped under the tree? Not likely. That too is good because we did that out of love. I hope they remember Christmas stockings being opened on mom and dad's bed and the camera flash going off as they walked into the living-room in their brand new pajamas.

What do I want them to remember? I pray that they remember the gift that was born and that we celebrate on Christmas day. I pray that they continue to cherish that Christmas gift for the rest of their lives and in turn that this belief becomes a tradition for their children. I pray that they remember the gift they received on the cross and that each day they open that gift in their heart to remind them that they are loved. I pray that they remember to re-gift this love as often as they are given the opportunity.

At this time of year when everything takes on a special meaning, I pray that my family knows the special feeling that comes not from gifts or cookies or parties but from knowing the King of Kings, the Lord of Lords. I pray that they know personally the gift that was born in the manger and died on the cross for them.

Steve Macdonald

Steve is Supervisor of Rail Cars and Shops for the TTC. Steve and Debbie and daughters Heather and Hayley are long term residents of Brampton. Steve enjoys playing organized hockey.

ChristMyths – Facts and Fictions

Continued from page 45

> *"Do not be afraid, Mary, you have found favor with God. You will be with child and give birth to a son, and you are to give him the name Jesus. He will be great and will be called the Son of the Most High. The Lord God will give him the throne of his father David, and he will reign over the house of Jacob forever; his kingdom will never end."*

Mary was upset – just like Joseph was upset. This couple didn't expect these events at all. Apparently Mary's reaction was fear because the angel had to tell her not to experience fear. God had actually favoured her with a magnificent role – an ordinary young woman performing a unique role for all of humanity. At least both

Tradition: Christmas Stockings

Since 1870 children have hung Christmas stockings in various places – at the ends of their beds or along the mantelpiece above the fireplace. The fantasy was perpetuated that Father Christmas or Santa Claus would fill them with gifts if they had been good for the year. If not they might just get a single lump of coal. The myth says that Father Christmas once dropped some gold coins while descending the chimney. But fortunately the coins were captured in stockings that had been hung out to dry. Children still hang stockings and magically find them full of gifts on Christmas morning.

Mary and Joseph had independent confirmation of what to name this baby.

But the angel's statement is much weightier than simply supplying a special name. The angel explains that he will be 1. the Son of the Most High 2. the Lord God will give him David's right to rule 3. his rule will last forever and 4. he will possess a kingdom that never ends. It is only to be understood at a still future time the complete significance of this rule. Many have rejected the option of following Jesus in the here and now because they fail to see the exhibition of that rulership in terms they grasp. This is not a book

Continued on page 48

The Story of the Candy Cane

A candy man wished to make a Christmas gift of Christ!
A gift straight from his heart!
First he shaped the candy
Into a shepherd's staff like a J.

The J stood for Jesus!
He used white stripes for Jesus' virgin birth.
Then He used red stripes for the blood of Jesus.
He called it a candy cane!
It was to remind us that Christmas was a sweet gift of love – that is Jesus!

Cassidy Burton

Cassidy is the oldest of three Burton children (sister to Kaiya and Carleigh) and daughter of Chris and Sara. She loves school and is a catcher for the Mississauga Tigers rep team.

ChristMyths – Facts and Fictions

Continued from page 47

about the Kingdom of God; it is about the Christmas story. Therefore it would be out of place to answer the age old query of, "If God is so good then why is there evil persisting in this world? And why did God even allow evil in the first place?" Those are important questions for another day. There are satisfying answers for those who have ears to hear. Those answers are found in the pages of the Bible.

> ### Fact: Christmas Eve 1914
>
> During World War I when Christmas arrived, at midnight Christmas eve the fighting stopped. A German brass band began playing Christmas carols. On Christmas morning the soldiers came out of their trenches and approached each other calling out "Merry Christmas." After overcoming initial misgivings they approached each other and shook hands. The friendliness continued as they exchanged some gifts, sang carols and other songs together. They lived in a truce for only a few days and even had a game of soccer before returning to the ugly business of war.

Questions

Mary had her questions too.

> "'How will this be,' Mary asked the angel, 'since I am a virgin?' The angel answered, 'The Holy Spirit will come upon you, and the power of the Most High will overshadow you. So the holy one to be born will be called the Son of God.'"

When you carefully look at the words here you can see that this miraculous conception has not yet occurred. In the passage from Matthew Mary is already pregnant. But in both cases the impossible is stated as actual. Of course a virgin birth is impossible. It was impossible to Mary as it is to us. It required something beyond the realm of human experience; it required the intervention of

Continued on page 50

A Two Way Street

As Christmas time is upon us, we have an opportunity once again to celebrate Jesus' birth. This gives me hope as a follower of Jesus Christ which I would like to share with you.

First of all, Christianity is so realistic. Jesus never claimed you could live without sin. That's why He was born. He died for our sins so we can go to heaven. He made us a promise which is outlined beautifully in Acts 3:38, *"Therefore, my brothers, I want you to know that through Jesus the forgiveness of sins is proclaimed to you."* All He really asks in return is that we turn from sin, believe in Him, and share what He has said in the Bible. Not a bad deal for a trip to heaven, eh? Jesus is honest with us too; He doesn't claim it will be easy. He gives us many tools to help us such as what He has said in the Bible, the Holy Spirit to fill our hearts and guide us, the power of prayer when we need help, and the love and support of other followers of Christ in a church. God loved us a lot to give us all that. His love for us was boundless when he sent his Son to die on the cross for us. We see this in Romans 5:8, *"But God demonstrates his own love for us in this: While we were still sinners, Christ died for us."*

Secondly, I have also learned that there are many forms of temptation. These are tools used by Satan to confound us, to tempt us, to turn us from what is right. I know that Satan is always at work. He puts a sugar coating on his work to make desire, greed, lust for power, seem right and good.

Recently I found a journal from 1982 which recorded struggles I was having then with temptation. I had written on March 22 of that year, "Everyday I am tempted in some way. It's easy to pray for help – and I always get it. Then I forget about the problem. Soon, I realize that the temptation is back stronger than ever." Today I decided to think about this. I know when I am tempted I can pray but I am also weak. Matthew 26:41 gives a warning, *"Watch and pray so that you will not fall into temptation. The spirit is willing, but the body is weak."* I also know the Holy Spirit is at work in my prayers. Romans 8:26 is encouraging when it says, *"In the same way, the Spirit helps us in our weakness. We do not know what we ought to*

Continued on page 52

God. Notice the three persons mentioned here. 1. The Holy Spirit 2. The Most High and 3. the Son of God. No wonder this put Mary into overload. All that divine power engaging her in the process of redemption.

The angel declares,

> *"For nothing is impossible with God."*

> ### Custom: Gift Giving
>
> Gift giving at Christmas is not just an engine of commercialism! Various customs and dates for Christmas vary from place to place. In various traditions the gifts are allegedly delivered by elves, angels, the Christ Child and even by Jesus' camel. But reality hits when the credit card bills arrive no matter the tradition.

The record then states,

> *"'I am the Lord's servant,' Mary answered. 'May it be to me as you have said.' Then the angel left her."*

It is pretty clear that Mary came to this angelic visitation with a prior commitment to being the Lord's servant. And with amazing resolve she agrees to this uncertain and unprecedented future.

The story continues with Mary's interaction with her cousin prior to the birth of Jesus. We will have to leave that beautiful part of the story for another time.

We pick the plot up again in chapter 2 of Luke. This is perhaps the most well known part of the birth narration.

It's History

Luke demonstrates his precision with historical facts.

Continued from page 50

pray for, but the Spirit himself intercedes for us with groans that words cannot express." But why was the temptation returning again and again after I prayed? I soon realized there was nothing wrong with the prayer process, but my approach to it. I needed to allow prayer to become an ongoing and consistent part of my life, because temptation certainly was! I began to see what kind of a relationship I could have with Jesus through prayer. He is my hope and life doesn't have to be so hard.

The Bible tells us in Matthew 10:28, *"Do not be afraid of those who kill the body but cannot kill the soul. Rather, be afraid of the One who can destroy both soul and body in hell."* So what if we don't just do the bad stuff? Is that enough? James 4:17 remarks, *"Anyone, then, who knows the good he ought to do and doesn't do it, sins."* The good news is we are not alone – remember the promise? 1 John 2:1 *"My dear children, I write this to you so that you will not sin. But if anybody does sin, we have one who speaks to the Father in our defense – Jesus Christ, the Righteous One."* Now that doesn't mean we have a "get out of jail free card." We do have to repent which is just a fancy way to say change by turning from evil and believe. We have to try. If we are not sincere, our prayers for forgiveness will not be heard. He knows what is in our hearts. Acts 3:19 says, *"Repent, then, and turn to God, so that your sins may be wiped out, that times of refreshing may come from the Lord."*

Our relationship with Jesus is a two way street. He loves us and wants us to be with Him; when we turn away it hurts Him. We see His grief at not being able to redeem us. I am astounded that Jesus suffered the agony He did on the cross, knowing so many would reject him. That's LOVE, and I for one will try not to throw His gifts back in his face. I would be a liar if I said I will always succeed in avoiding temptation. That is the struggle, but it is worth it.

Here, then, is the reason I celebrate the birth of Jesus, and have hope as one of His followers. It's overwhelming to know Jesus loved me that much. It's good to know He wants me to gain eternal life in heaven. I rejoice in the fact that I'm not alone! You know we are significant when you see statements like this from

Continued on page 54

ChristMyths – Facts and Fictions

Continued from page 51

> *"In those days Caesar Augustus issued a decree that a census should be taken of the entire Roman world. (This was the first census that took place while Quirinius was governor of Syria.) And everyone went to his own town to register."*

This set the course for a stressful trip from the north in Nazareth down to Joseph's ancestral home – Bethlehem.

> *"So Joseph also went up from the town of Nazareth in Galilee to Judea, to Bethlehem the town of David, because he belonged to the house and line of David. He went there to register with Mary, who was pledged to be married to him and was expecting a child. While they were there, the time came for the baby to be born, and she gave birth to her firstborn, a son. She wrapped him in cloths and placed him in a manger, because there was no room for them in the inn."*

Fiction: Mistletoe

This plant is actually a parasite that lives high up in trees, feeding on the life juices of its host. According to Norse mythology, Balder, the god of the summer sun was killed with an arrow dipped in mistletoe. His mother, Frigga, cried so long that the berries turned from white to red. Balder came back to life. His mother was so happy and started kissing everyone underneath it. She declared it a sacred plant to symbolize love rather than death. Today kissing under the mistletoe is a fun, festive tradition.

In this one simple paragraph we have the entire story of the actual birth of Jesus. This is the moment. The event is so simply stated. All that we have gathered around that story is uninspired embellishment. There is no mention of the halo or glow so many artists have added. There is no mention of a stable or a cave. However, it is a reasonable assumption that an eating trough for animals would be located in such a structure. And there are no animals mentioned. There are a whole range of possible options. We don't know. Maybe they just grabbed a manger and stuck it under an

Continued on page 55

Continued from page 52

Luke 15:7, *"I tell you that in the same way there will be more rejoicing in heaven over one sinner who repents than over ninety-nine righteous persons who do not need to repent."* I have faith and hope when I read Hebrews 9:28, *"... so Christ was sacrificed once to take away the sins of many people; and he will appear a second time, not to bear sin, but to bring salvation to those who are waiting for him."* I'll be waiting for Him, and I pray that you will join me.

I leave you with this last powerful statement to think about from 1 John 1 5-10, *"This is the message we have heard from him and declare to you: God is light; in him there is no darkness at all. If we claim to have fellowship with him yet walk in the darkness, we lie and do not live by the truth. But if we walk in the light, as he is in the light, we have fellowship with one another, and the blood of Jesus, his Son, purifies us from all sin. If we claim to be without sin, we deceive ourselves and the truth is not in us. If we confess our sins, he is faithful and just and will forgive us our sins and purify us from all unrighteousness. If we claim we have not sinned, we make him out to be a liar and his word has no place in our lives."*

Howie Johnson

Howie is a husband to Sheila and father to Ryan. He loves to help others and hang out at his cottage near Perry Sound.

ChristMyths – Facts and Fictions

Continued from page 53

olive tree for protection. We just know they couldn't get a room in the singular inn referred to. We don't have a donkey ride from Nazareth as reasonable as an assumption that may be. We just have Mary, Joseph and the birth of Jesus. Simple detail about Mary wrapping the baby up and laying him down in the simple available place.

> ### Tradition: Candles
>
> Centuries ago candles were offered as gifts and used to ward off darkness both physical and spiritual. The first use of candles at Christmas was during the Roman festival of Saturnalia.
>
> In some places candles were placed in the front window and the fantasy was that they would guide the Christ Child as he wandered from house to house on Christmas Eve.

Doesn't that seem strange to you? All this promise of a kingship and he is laid where? He is clothed in what? And there was nobody in town to take pity on a regal child? Go figure.

But take note. If you were going to make up a story of a coming king you wouldn't write it that way and neither would I. The story is unbelievable. And that is one of the simple things that actually makes it so believable. The beginning of a life story that ends with no visible signs normally associated with the kingship of some small offshore island nation let alone the story of the King of the ages. You can't make this stuff up! This must be the truth!

The Shepherds

So now the story moves to its final phase. Well that is in Luke's portion of it. We already dealt with Matthew's part which when intertwined gives us the composite.

Continued on page 57

Jesus

Loving, Merciful

Teaching, Preaching, Healing

Son, Way, Truth, Life

Eternal, Blameless

Offered, Hated, Saved

King, Saviour, Holy Spirit

Kaiya Burton

Kaiya is the middle child of three Burton children (sister to Cassidy and Carleigh) and daughter of Chris and Sara. Kaiya runs the computer and display for The Breakfast Church.

"And there were shepherds living out in the fields nearby, keeping watch over their flocks at night. An angel of the Lord appeared to them, and the glory of the Lord shone around them, and they were terrified. But the angel said to them, 'Do not be afraid. I bring you good news of great joy that will be for all the people. Today in the town of David a Savior has been born to you; he is Christ the Lord. This will be a sign to you: You will find a baby wrapped in cloths and lying in a manger.'"

Fiction: Angels

It is common to believe that angels are departed humans who look over us. However, the Bible teaches that angels are another class of being created by God. They appear occasionally in the Bible narrative as "ministering spirits." They are wingless creatures. The description of the angel at the resurrection from Matthew 28:2-3 supplies this description: *"... for an angel of the Lord came down from heaven and, going to the tomb, rolled back the stone and sat on it. His appearance was like lightning, and his clothes were white as snow."*

Think about it – shepherds? These were the minimum wage night shift guys. They don't form the who's who list of celebrity endorsers. You can make what you will of the choice – and many good points could be made. But Luke is just telling it as it happened.

One Angel

It starts with one angel. Now lest you think all the primitive people were used to inventing angel visitors remember that every time an angel shows up people get upset. This time we have something not mentioned before. *"The glory of the Lord shone around them ..."* When the angel appeared there was something else in this case. There is no record that the angel was floating in the sky. At other times angelic appearances have them on the ground so there is no need

God Gave

At one of our weekly Home Group meetings at Heartland Fellowship (The Breakfast Church), all the participants shared their favourite Bible passages. Putting them all together we came up with a "Christmas" theme that became this song, *God Gave*. Christmas time is so busy and focused on giving. But without the depth and sacrifice of God's love when He gave his Son our lives would not be so rich.

When we meditate on the words of *God Gave* we focus on how we did not deserve or earn anything.

When we consider the lengths at which God took to communicate with us we cannot help but change our perspective.

Five very different Scripture writers spoke at five very different points in history in five very different ways. However the underlying message comes through loud and clear that *God Gave*.

This is a humbling message that we must remember. This humbling message changes how we act and how we speak to those around us. The best gift we can give our friends, family members and anyone else we come in contact with is that God also gave to them. What lengths can we take to communicate that?

John 3:16-17:

> *"For God so loved the world that he gave his one and only Son, whoever believes in him shall not perish but have eternal life. For God did not send his Son into the world to condemn the world, but to save the world through him."*

Philippians 2:5-11:

> *"Your attitude should be the same as that of Christ Jesus: Who, being in very nature, did not consider equality with God something to be grasped, but made himself nothing, taking the very nature a servant, being made in human likeness. And being found in appearance as a man, he humbled himself and became obedient to*

Continued on page 60

ChristMyths – Facts and Fictions

Continued from page 57

to think of it as otherwise. The angel voices words (not music). The message is clear. For the first time the word Christ comes from an angel's lips. Here we have a *"Savior"* – the one who brings salvation. And incidentally, later in his life Jesus repeatedly states that he is the only source of salvation. If he was wrong he is either a lunatic or a liar. But if he is right he lives up to his advanced billing as *"Christ the Lord."* And so that the shepherds would be sure they found the correct baby, the incredible birth circumstances of the baby's wrapping and the manger are set out for them.

Tradition: Turkey Dinner

For centuries in the British Isles the traditional meal was goose or the head of a boar. This changed in the sixteenth century when the turkey was introduced to England. In 1526 a trader imported six turkey birds from the colonies in America.

The bird soon became popular because of its unique taste. Turkey became the traditional English Christmas meal, served with stuffing, cranberry sauce and bread sauce along with roast potatoes, Yorkshire pudding, brussel sprouts, peas and parsnips.

A Multitude of Angels

Then the story gets big.

> *"Suddenly a great company of the heavenly host appeared with the angel, praising God and saying, 'Glory to God in the highest, and on earth peace to men on whom his favor rests.'"*

Again, maybe they sang but the emphasis is on the lyrics if they did. Notice this magnificent intertwining of the experience of God in the highest and people living in this messy world. That is

Continued on page 61

Continued from page 58

death – even death on a cross! Therefore God exalted him to the highest place and gave him the name that is above every name, that at the name of Jesus every knee should bow, in heaven and on earth and under the earth, and every tongue confess that Jesus Christ is Lord, to the glory of God the Father."

Ecclesiastes 12: 13-14:

"Now all has been heard; here is the conclusion of the matter: Fear God and keep his commandments, for this is the whole duty of man. For God will bring every deed into judgment, including every hidden thing, whether it is good or evil."

Lamentations 3:19-23:

"I remember my affliction and my wandering, the bitterness and the gall. I well remember them and my soul is downcast within me. Yet this I call to mind and therefore I have hope: Because of the LORD's great love we are not consumed, for his compassions never fail. They are new every morning; great is your faithfulness."

Psalm 40:2-4:

"He lifted me out of the slimy pit, out of the mud and mire; he set my feet on a rock and gave me a firm place to stand. He put a new song in my mouth, a hymn of praise to our God. Many will see and fear and put their trust in the LORD. Blessed is the man who makes the LORD his trust, who does not look to the proud, to those who turn aside to false gods."

God Gave

God gave
God gave
God gave the world His Son
God gave
God gave
God gave His only Son.

Because He loved the world

Continued on page 62

Continued from page 59

the glory of the Christmas message that is as relevant today as then. As Paul later puts it,

> *"All this is from God, who reconciled us to himself through Christ and gave us the ministry of reconciliation: that God was reconciling the world to himself in Christ, not counting men's sins against them. And he has committed to us the message of reconciliation. We are therefore Christ's ambassadors, as though God were making his appeal through us. We implore you on Christ's behalf: Be reconciled to God."*

Fiction: World Peace

At Christmas time we hear many say that the message of Christmas has something to do with bringing peace on earth. This concept is developed from a misunderstanding of the angel message to the shepherds which was translated in the Authorized Version of the Bible published in 1611 as *"Glory to God in the highest, and on earth peace, good will toward men."* This has been misunderstood as a message from man to man to encourage peaceful living. That is a laudable goal but what the angels were saying is better translated as, *"Glory to God in the highest, and on earth peace to men on whom his favor rests."* The message is not about peace between peoples; it is about the new and living way of having peace between God and people. That is a very different message. It is further born out by Jesus saying during his ministry, *"Do not suppose that I have come to bring peace to the earth. I did not come to bring peace, but a sword."* By that he was referring to the division of misunderstanding even within families when people chose to follow him.

Read it for yourself in Matthew 10:32-39.

It is the offer of peace when any person accepts the message and is reconciled to God. It is not a promise of automatic peace. Personal inner peace comes when a person is rightly related to God through Jesus the only mediator. Paul put it this way in 1 Timothy 2:5-6,

Continued on page 63

Continued from page 60

God did not spare His Son
He gave Him up for us all.
It was a less than modest birth,
A more than grievous death
God gave His only Son

Remember the One who made you.
Remember the One who gave.
Remember His love and find hope.
Remember His commandments.
Remember His faithfulness.
For He has loved us all.

I believe and I live.
I have a new song in my heart
About the greatest gift of life.
His love is for you.
Just believe and you'll live.
Christmas has new meaning for you.

God gave
God gave
God gave the world His Son
God gave
God gave
God gave His only Son.

Sara Burton and Fred Brown

Continued from page 61

> *"For there is one God and one mediator between God and men, the man Christ Jesus, who gave himself as a ransom for all men – the testimony given in its proper time."*

The requirement is a simple submission of all thought, belief, feeling, behaviour and choice to the ultimate King. Simple but so profound!

Continuation

And then the birth story concludes.

> *"So they hurried off and found Mary and Joseph, and the baby, who was lying in the manger. When they had seen him, they spread the word concerning what had been told them about this child, and all who heard it were amazed at what the shepherds said to them. But Mary treasured up all these things and pondered them in her heart. The shepherds returned, glorifying and praising God for all the things they had heard and seen, which were just as they had been told."*

The shepherds found the right baby with his parents. Then they simply told others about this child. We don't know how the shepherds behaved in the presence of the baby. But we do know they were impressed so much that they spread the news. We also know there was a new possession in their hearts. Was it joy? Was it hope? Was it discovery? Was it more than all that? Whatever it was it turned their hearts to glorifying and praising God. They didn't simply adore the Son; they praised the God who sent him.

That's it. There are no more authoritative facts to tell you about. The Bible has spoken and that part of the message has been completed.

But that is just the spectacular beginning. Won't you give the complete message a chance? Read it for yourself. Matthew, Mark, Luke or John or all four. Each see the story from a slightly different perspective. But the actual unfolding life of Jesus will astound you.

Continued on page 65

Yeshua is Here

Yeshua God is salvation.
Yeshua is Jesus our Saviour.
Yeshua God is salvation.
Yeshua is Jesus our Saviour.

Good news! Yeshua is here! Good news! Yeshua is here!

To God be the glory forever.
To God be the glory forever.
To God be the glory forever.
To God be the glory forever..

Good news! Yeshua is here! Good news! Yeshua is here!

He's turned to us with mercy.
He's turned to us with mercy.
He's turned to us with mercy.
He's turned to us with mercy.

Amen! Yeshua is here!
Amen! Yeshua is here!

Sara Burton

Isaiah 12:2

> *"Surely God is my salvation; I will trust and not be afraid. The LORD, the LORD, is my strength and my song; he has become my salvation."*

There has been a lot of extraneous noise added to the Christmas season over the years. And it is fun! But won't you please cut through the tinsel and consider the facts? And then when you do look at the history you are likely to experience what so many millions of others have known. There is a wonderful attraction and soul satisfaction that grows as you ponder. Your heart will be strangely warmed. Your ability to make choices will be challenged to make a new set of choices. You have the option to give into the noise and spend your time this season with the latest ChristMyth. It may keep you fueled up with pleasant sensations until the New Year.

ChristMyths will never satisfy your soul. Knowing the Christ of Christmas will. If you want some help in finding out more any of the participants in this book can help show you the way.

Personally, I am always open to friendly dialogue on a variety of subjects but the one that matters most to me is the unfolding story of the life of Christ and all that he means to me. Give me a call any time and we will sit down over a cup of coffee or tea and share our individual perspectives.

Gary Carter

Gary is the part-time Pastor of Heartland Fellowship, a writer and the President of Kainos International Ministries. One sample of Kainos' global work is support for an orphanage in Myanmar.

Made in the USA
Charleston, SC
10 December 2009